MW01041603

GOD
THE FINAL FRONTIER

POSITIVE PROOF FOR HIS EXISTENCE AND HIS LOVE

By
Philip DelRe

Voice Publishing
A Division of
Voice in the Wilderness Ministries
Belvidere, Illinois 61008 USA

God the Final Frontier
Positive Proof for His Existence and His Love
Philip DelRe

Copyright © 2012 by Voice Publishing
A Division of Voice in the Wilderness Ministries
9757 Squire Lane
Belvidere, Illinois USA
All Rights Reserved.

Scripture taken from The New King James Bible
Copyright © 1982 by Thomas Nelson, Inc.
Used by permission

ISBN 0-9677520-8-6
ISBN 978-0-9677520-8-2
Third printing, August 2015
Printed in the United States of America

Please visit our website for other helpful resources:
www.voice-wilderness.org

More than 50,000 copies in print

Table of Contents

Chapter One

The Wonders of God's Creation

Try to imagine nothing exists. There is no sun, no moon, no stars, and no galaxies. There are no elements such as carbon, hydrogen, nitrogen, or oxygen. There are no such things as time, space, matter, or energy. There is no universe, no God, nothing.

If there ever was a time when nothing existed, then nothing would exist now, therefore something must be eternal.

You have only two choices: Either God is eternal and uncreated, or matter is eternal and uncreated. There is no third option. It was 1910 when Albert Einstein published his Theory of Relativity. This mathematical equation (math being a perfect science) provided a basis for proof that time, space, and matter were not eternal, but had a beginning.

Although the Bible was written thousands of years before the genesis of scientific research, amazingly, Einstein's discovery fit the biblical account of creation perfectly. The very first verse in the Bible says,

In the beginning God created the Heavens and the earth.

In the beginning (that's time), God created (that's energy) the heavens (that's space), and the earth (that's matter). That's quite a coincidence!

Einstein Didn't Invent Physics — He Discovered It

Einstein's equation (Energy equals Mass times the speed of light squared) left him (and all the rest of us) staring in the face of God. This formula proved that the universe was not eternal (as Einstein supposed), but had a definite point in time when it began. That leaves us with our only other option,

God is Eternal and Uncreated

As Norman Geisler writes in his excellent book, *I Don't Have Enough Faith to be an Atheist,* "Asking the question, 'Where did God come from?' is a nonsensical question. It contains the false assumption that God was created or had a beginning, and then asks—how is that possible? It would be better to ask,

Why is there something rather than nothing?"

The question itself ("where did God come from?") is fatally flawed. Geisler put it this way, "It's like asking: Where did the bachelor get his wife? Or, what does blue sound like?" Bachelors by definition do not have wives, and blue is not in the category of sound. In the same sense, God is not in the category of created things!

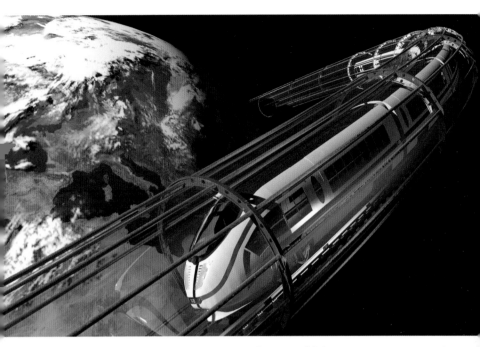

Try to Wrap Your Mind Around This

How could time have a beginning? Suppose time went backwards indefinitely, so there was no first day. If time just kept going back and back with no starting point, then this day (today) could never arrive. But this day is here. Therefore there had to be a first day, and that was the day time began.

The Laws of Nature

Scientific analyses would be impossible without uniformity in nature. Time, space, and matter must be uniform in order for scientific experimentation to be meaningful.

The physical laws that govern the known universe are so constant that astronomers can chart the position of stars, moons, planets, and even comets far into the future with accuracy and precision.

Time is based on the uniformity of our solar system. The earth rotates at a constant speed of 1,000 miles an hour while simultaneously revolving around the sun. At 67,000 miles an hour, earth makes the 584 million mile journey once every 365.25 days. Its "on time" arrival record is better than any train or airline in the world!

"Our limited minds cannot grasp the mysterious force that moves the constellations." —Albert Einstein

The Wonders of the Milky Way Galaxy

The Milky Way Galaxy is 100,000 light years across, and 10,000 light years in diameter. To get from one end of the galaxy to the other, you would need to travel at the speed of light, 186,282 miles per second (which is 670,616,629 mph). That speed would take you around the world 7.5 times in one second!

The earth is 26,000 light years from the center of the galaxy. If you were to take a commercial airliner from earth to the center of our own galaxy, traveling at 550 miles an hour, it would take you not 278 million, billion, trillion, or quadrillion years, but 278 quintillion years to get there. One quintillion is a thousand quadrillion!

Not only do all the planets in our solar system revolve around the sun, but the entire Milky Way Galaxy is revolving (along with its 100–400 billion stars). It will take 250 million years to make one complete revolution!

As passengers on starship earth, we are at this moment spinning around the center of the Milky Way Galaxy like a giant cosmic Ferris wheel. Our speed is 558,000 miles an hour.

What is this "mysterious force" that moves the constellations? What causes the entire galaxy to rotate? What holds the stars in place? Why don't they collide? How much power is required to spin the galaxy while holding 100 billion stars in place?

Einstein knew that someone or something was responsible for this mind blowing phenomenon. The Bible provided answers to these and other questions long ago. In Isaiah 40:26 we read,

> Lift up your eyes on high, and see who has created these things, Who brings out their host by number; He calls them all by name, by the greatness of His might and the strength of His power; not one is missing.

In creation, God provided observable evidence of His omnipotence, so everyone could see a sample His glory. Psalm 19:1-3 says,

> The heavens declare the glory of God; and the firmament shows His handiwork. Day unto day utters speech, and night unto night reveals knowledge. There is no speech nor language where their voice is not heard.

In other words, all a thinking person has to do is take a good look at the sun, moon, stars, and his or her own body to *know* that anything so complex, so perfectly designed and well balanced, could in no way have made itself.

A Rocket Scientist Tells it Like It Is

Robert Jastrow, an astrophysicist and former Director of the National Aeronautics and Space Administrations Goddard Institute, in his book *God and the Astronomers*, writes,

> At this moment it seems as though science will never be able to raise the curtain on the mystery of creation. For the scientist who has lived by his faith in the power of reason, the story ends like a bad dream. He has scaled the mountains of ignorance; he is about to conquer the highest peak; as he pulls himself over the final rock, he is greeted by a band of theologians who have been sitting there for centuries.

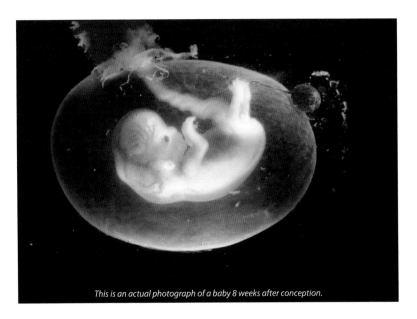

This is an actual photograph of a baby 8 weeks after conception.

Just for Fun

Which is more complex? The world's fastest supercomputer, the world's most advanced robotic system, the Space Shuttle, or an earthworm? Answer: Nobody knows how to make a worm! A single cell contains millions of little machines that work together to make proteins. No scientist has ever produced a machine that can even begin to compare to the complexity and efficiency of one DNA cell. Computers, robots, and rocket-ships all require intelligent designers, so do worms.

You Are God's Greatest Miracle

On that glorious day of conception amazing things began to happen. Two cells became one and then, *miraculously*, the one became two! Beginning as a single cell, you began to divide exponentially, and on the day you were born your completed body was made up of more than 100 trillion extremely complex, machines called cells. One hundred and fifty years ago (before we had electron microscopes), Charles Darwin mistakenly believed that cells were simple. Today, we *know* that one DNA cell is the most densely packed and elaborate assembly of detailed information in the known universe!

Your heart began to beat when you were only 22 days old. At three weeks we could see your eyes and ears. At six weeks we could see your fingers and toes. At 11 weeks you could smile, frown, and suck your thumb. On the day you were born, you were nine months old.

Consider how Psalm 139:14-16 describes God's glory,

> I praise you because I am fearfully and wonderfully made; your works are wonderful, I know that full well. My frame was not hidden from you when I was made in the secret place, when I was woven together in the depths of the earth. Your eyes saw my unformed body; all the days ordained for me were written in your book before one of them came to be.

The Human Brain

The human brain is the most complex thing known to science. It is made up of some one hundred billion cells which connect to ten other cells. That is one trillion connections, ten times more than the estimated number of stars in the Milky Way galaxy!

Everything you have ever experienced is stored in the memory banks of your brain. Your earliest childhood memories—playing with a friend, a birthday party, a kind word, a walk in the park, or a gift.

By contrast, the fastest supercomputer in the world cost 100 million dollars, is as large as a 6,000 square foot house, and it still cannot produce one original thought.

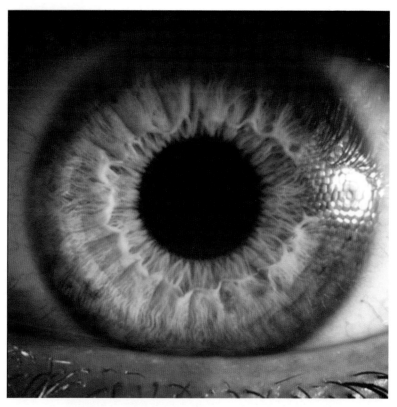

Would You Sell Your Eyes for a Million Dollars?

Have you seen the awesome beauty of the stars, the wonderful colors of a rainbow, the majesty of the Grand Canyon, children playing in a park, or the look of love?

Your eye has 137 million, light-sensitive cells (cameras) that translate everything you see instantaneously to the brain, and your brain sees!

In Exodus 4:11-12 God says,

> So the Lord said to him, "Who has made man's mouth? Or who makes the mute, the deaf, the seeing, or the blind? Have not I, the Lord?"

The Nose Knows

Your nose is so sensitive, it can distinguish between more than 10,000 different aromas: from freshly brewed coffee, to apples and oranges, to fruits and flowers.

Highly sophisticated and super sensitive receptor cells in your nose detect vaporized chemicals in the air. Familiar aromas can impact your emotions as you smell dinner cooking, and even bring back memories of people, places, or events from the past—the nose knows.

What Makes Food so Enjoyable?

There are 10,000 taste buds in your tongue and in the roof of your mouth. That is what makes eating so enjoyable. The digestive system then breaks down the food, extracts the nutrients which are absorbed by the blood. The blood delivers the nutrients to the cells, which are transformed into energy.

The Ability to Speak

Unlike animals, man is made in the image of God. One of the attributes we share with our Creator is the ability to speak (and even sing). This is both a privilege and a responsibility. Not surprisingly, God's Word says we will be held accountable for every word we speak.

You are what you are and you are where you are in large part because of what has come out of your mouth. You can change what you are and where you are by changing what you say and how you say it. Some of the most beautiful words in any language are, "I was wrong; please forgive me; I love you." In Proverbs 18:21, King Solomon said,

> Death and life are in the power of the tongue, and those who love it will eat its fruit.

Do You Enjoy Music?

Can you appreciate great music like Beethoven's 5th Symphony, or that special someone saying the words, "I love you?" How about the sound of wind blowing through the trees on a cool summer night, birds in the morning, or the ocean waves?

Incredibly, your ears contain 24,000 fibers, much like the strings on a piano. But, this design is far more sophisticated since a concert piano only has 88 strings. The shorter, thinner fibers in your ear receive and transmit the high frequencies, and the longer, thicker fibers deliver the low frequencies.

These very fine and extremely sensitive fibers transmit sound waves to the brain, which detects the pitch, tone, volume, direction, and distance.

Consider what you would miss if you could not hear the sound of the human voice, or the beauty of music. How much do you think a deaf person might give to hear the amazing sounds we take for granted?

The Amazing Strength of the Human Heart

This amazing machine called your heart is about the same size as your fist. Through electrical impulses, the heart pumps oxygen and nutrient rich blood through more than 60,000 miles of vessels, veins and arteries. If lined up end to end, that is enough to go around the world almost three times!

The heart expands and contracts up to 100,000 times per day. Imagine trying to do 100,000 push-ups a day. The heart pumps five quarts of blood a minute, which amounts to 2,000 gallons a day. Imagine trying to carry 2,000 gallons of water for 60,000 miles every day! Your heart does it from 1,000 to 1,500 times a day, depending on how much you exercise!

How energy efficient is the human body? The whole system can run on bread and water!

Your respiratory system works automatically, supplying the blood with oxygen as you breathe. Your central nervous system is comprised of the brain and spinal cord.

Your skeletal system comprises your bones, tendons, ligaments, and cartilage. The skeleton is composed of 270 bones at birth—but decreases to 206 after some bones fuse together by adulthood.

Bone marrow is where new cells are constantly replenished. Your immune system consists of a vast network of cells, tissues, and organs that work as a team to destroy disease-causing, free radicals.

The male and female reproductive systems are incredibly complex systems of organs that work together to produce the miracle of life!

The human brain (the most complex thing known to science) has more than 600 muscles under its command. Divided into two groups, voluntary muscles work only when instructed to, like when you play the guitar, throw a football, or walk. Involuntary muscles control your heart beat, breathing, and cause your eyes to blink.

You have more than 30 facial muscles which cause you to: smile, frown, and create looks of surprise, sadness, confusion, anger, wonder, joy, peace, and love.

The marble sculpture of Moses (above) is simple compared to the human body, yet no one in his right mind would claim this magnificent sculpture happened by chance. It is the work of one of the greatest artists of all time—Michelangelo (1475–1574). But, it doesn't walk, talk, think, speak, or, have the ability to recreate itself. You do.

The Mona Lisa proves beyond the-shadow-of-a-doubt there was a Leonardo da Vinci. The Sistine Chapel is positive proof there was a Michelangelo. And, the 5th Symphony is empirical proof there was a Ludwig van Beethoven. These marvels of talent and ingenuity don't happen by chance.

Even though none of us has ever actually seen these great artists, no judge, jury (or scientist) in the world would disagree that these masterpieces prove their creators existed.

You Are Priceless

Michelangelo produced many paintings as did Leonardo da Vinci. The 5th Symphony was one of many produced by Ludwig van Beethoven. These works of art have value because they were produced by great masters and are few in number. But, there is only one of you and not another will ever be produced. You are one of the rarest things in the world.

What the Mona Lisa was to Leonardo da Vinci, what the Sistine Chapel was to Michelangelo, and what the 5th Symphony was to Beethoven, you are to God. You are God's masterpiece, and the crown of His creation!

> For as a young man marries a virgin, so shall your sons marry you; And as the bridegroom rejoices over the bride, so shall your God rejoice over you (Isa. 62:5).

Romans 1:20 says,

> For since the creation of the world His invisible attributes are clearly seen, being understood by the things that are made, even His eternal power and divine nature so men are without excuse.

Chapter Two

The Word of God, Living and Written

The Bible is utterly unique among all other books for several reasons. It not only claims to be "The Word of God," but offers many infallible proofs that it is.

The Bible answers the most profound questions beating in the human heart: Who am I? Where did I come from? Why am I here? Where am I going when I die?

Between its content, its unparalleled circulation, and its impact on the world, there is no possible term of comparison between the Bible, Jesus Christ, and any other so-called "holy book" or religious leader in history. Keep reading and you'll see why.

Just to make certain no one could ever claim the Bible was a man-made conspiracy, it was written over the course of 1,500 years, on three continents—Europe, Asia, and Africa.

It was written in three languages—Hebrew, Aramaic, and Greek—by 40 different writers. Although the writers were separated by more than 1,500 years, the Bible has a beginning, middle, and an end. The main theme is *Redemption*. And, the main character, from Genesis to Revelation, is Jesus Christ! Redemption literally means to buy a slave in order to set them free. In this case, it refers to freedom from the guilt, the power, and the penalty of sin!

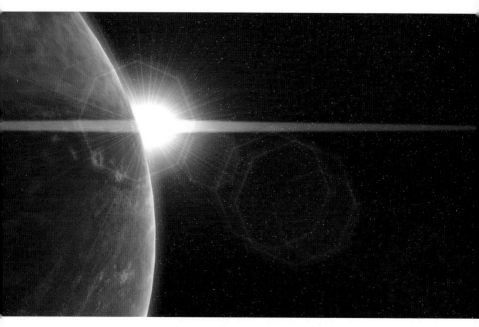

Astronomy and the Bible

- The ancient Egyptians believed that the earth was suspended on five pillars.

- The Greeks believed Atlas held the earth on his shoulders.

- The Hindus believed that the earth was held up by an elephant, the elephant was on a tortoise, the tortoise was on a serpent, and the serpent was swimming on a cosmic sea.

- And in *Surah* 18:84-92, the Koran says that the sun sets in a puddle of mud!

Until about 400 years ago, many people thought the earth was flat. In fact, the *Flat Earth Society* still does!

Yet in chapter 26 of Job, one of the oldest books in the Bible, we read,

God hangs the earth upon nothing.

In 750 B.C., the 40th chapter of Isaiah told us that,

God sits upon the circle of the earth.

One Word Proves the Bible Is True—Prophecy!

Bible prophecy is empirical proof the Scriptures are divinely inspired— proving God is the author. No human being can predict the future with 100 percent accuracy. Only someone with omniscience can do that! This is what God says of Himself in Isa. 44:6-7,

> Thus says the Lord, the King of Israel, and His Redeemer, the Lord of hosts: "I am the First and I am the Last; besides Me there is no God. And who can proclaim as I do? Then let him declare it and set it in order for Me, since I appointed the ancient people. And the things that are coming and shall come."

One recurring theme of biblical prophecy concerns one of the most strategic pieces of real estate on earth. Ezekiel 36-39 (written 2,500 years ago) speaks of the birth, death, and rebirth of the nation of Israel.

God said the Jewish people would be exiled from Israel (because of her sin), and the land would remain desolate for a long period of time. Then in the "latter days" they would return to become a nation once again.

As we look at history that is precisely what happened. In A.D. 70, the Roman Empire destroyed Jerusalem. The surviving Jews ran for their lives to the four corners of the earth. Miraculously, they remained a distinct race even though they had no homeland for nearly 1,900 years. Then, after World War II, they began to trickle (and eventually flood) back in to their "Promised Land." On May 14, 1948, a second Jewish state was established precisely as the Bible predicted!

The Day of the Lord

Israel is God's prophetic time-clock. Again and again the Scriptures tell us that the war to end all wars will be fought over Jerusalem-Israel. The ancient Scriptures refer to it as, "The War of Armageddon." In 2 Peter 3:10-13, we have a description of what appears to be a nuclear explosion. Amazingly, this was written by Peter more than 2,000 years ago.

> But the day of the Lord will come as a thief in the night, in which the heavens will pass away with a great noise, and the elements will melt with fervent heat; both the earth and the works that are in it will be burned up. Therefore, since all these things will be dissolved, what manner of persons ought you to be in holy conduct and godliness, looking for and hastening the coming of the day of God, because of which the heavens will be dissolved, being on fire, and the elements will melt with fervent heat? Nevertheless we,

according to His promise, look for new heavens and a new earth in which righteousness dwells.

Zechariah 12:1, 14:2, Matthew 24, Mark 13, Luke 21, and many other biblical passages spell out in precise detail what the conditions will be just prior to the return of Jesus Christ. In Matthew 24:4-14 Jesus tells us what they are,

> Take heed that no one deceives you. For many will come in My name, saying, "I am the Christ," and will deceive many. And you will hear of wars and rumors of wars. See that you are not troubled; for all these things must come to pass, but the end is not yet. For nation will rise against nation, and kingdom against kingdom. And there will be famines, pestilences, and earthquakes in various places. All these are the beginning of sorrows. Then they will deliver you up to tribulation and kill you, and you will be hated by all nations for My name's sake. And then many will be offended, will betray one another, and will hate one another. Then many false prophets will rise up and deceive many. And because lawlessness will abound, the love of many will grow cold. But he who endures to the end shall be saved. And this gospel of the kingdom will be preached in all the world as a witness to all the nations, and then the end will come.

That is precisely what we see happening right now. The Middle East is the most strategic and volatile region in the world today, and Israel is at the center of it all. How does the Bible know these things?

Do the Math

According to Ph.D. astrophysicists and other qualified American scientists, the odds of the Bible's more than 2,500 predictions being fulfilled by chance is one out of a number expressed as 1 with 2,000 zeros after it!

According to the mathematical science of probability, if a number has more than 50 zeros after it, the odds of that happening by chance make it virtually impossible. To put this in perspective, the number of atoms in the known universe is believed to be 10 to the 80th power, and one occurrence out of 10 to the 80th power amounts to zero. The Bible is true!

THE LIVING WORD OF GOD
Jesus Christ Is the Most Famous Person Who Ever Lived

We live in the 21st Century A.D. The A.D. is the abbreviation for the Latin words, "Anno Domni." Literally translated it means, "In the year of the Lord," i.e., the Lord Jesus Christ!

If you went backwards 4,000 years, we, the people of the common-era, refer to that as 2,000 B.C. That's 2,000 years "before Christ." And, why do we do that? Because 2,000 years ago a real historical person came to this planet and had such a profound impact on the world by what He said and by what He did the world marks time by His birth!

If God Came to Earth as a Man…

You would expect Him to say and do things that would distinguish Him from all other men. Jesus provides us with the greatest demonstration of authority, courage, conviction, wisdom, power, purity, and love the world has ever seen.

Let's look at the evidence. When you read the words of Jesus in the Gospels, you quickly realize that no one in history ever spoke like Jesus did.

Why Is It that the Name "Jesus" Can Clear Out a Room Faster Than Any Other Name in the World?

You can mention the names of any of these other so-called religious leaders, and no one gives a flip. Why is it that in many places of the world you can be imprisoned, tortured, dismembered, or murdered for teaching Christianity? All Jesus did was say things like,

> Love your enemies; if your enemy is hungry, feed him; if he is thirsty, give him a drink; if he takes your shirt, give him your coat, too (Matt. 5:40, 44; Rom. 12:20).

No one has ever spoken with that kind of love before or since. So, why is it that just the mention of the name Jesus causes so much discomfort and even hatred? The answer is found in John 3:19-20,

> And this is the condemnation, that the light has come into the world, and men loved darkness rather than light, because their deeds were evil. For everyone practicing evil hates the light and does not come to the light, lest his deeds should be exposed.

Just the mention of His name brings the conviction of sin. Paradoxically, the name of Jesus draws more people together every week around the world for worship than anyone else. Keep reading and you'll see why.

The Greatest Demonstration of Love the World Has Ever Seen

The teaching of Jesus could not have been more antithetical to the Roman Empire's idea of justice. In Matthew 5:44 Jesus said,

> I say to you, love your enemies, and pray for those who persecute you. If you only love those who love you, what reward do you have?

It is said that the Mafia love their family members, but kill their enemies. Jesus is saying in essence, "If you love only those who love you, how are you any different than the Mafia?"

When His enemies nailed Him to the cross, Jesus was naked and in unimaginable pain from head to toe. His accusers laughed, mocked, ridiculed, and spat at Him. Amazingly, 700 years earlier, Isaiah

53 prophesied that the Messiah would be despised, rejected, and crushed for the sin of the world.

Psalm 22 also predicts the crucifixion of Christ at least 1,000 years before the Romans developed it as a form of capital punishment.

The Roman soldiers were throwing dice at the foot of the cross to see who would keep His clothes. It was in that horrible humiliation and searing pain that Jesus prayed,

> Father, forgive them, for they know not what they do.

This concern for other people in the pain of death was so profound, so completely antithetical to human nature, the thief on His right (also being crucified) had a revelation—Jesus truly was divine. This dying man then cried out to Jesus,

> Lord, remember me when you come into your kingdom.

And Jesus replied,

> This day you shall be with Me in Paradise.

Who would make up such a story and expect anyone to believe it? Where else can you find a more compelling or authoritative demonstration of love in all of history? No mere man could have expressed such selfless love and concern for the eternal destiny of the very people who were responsible for His suffering.

You will not find this kind of sacrificial love in any other religion, philosophy, or system of thought.

As C.S. Lewis So Eloquently Pointed Out, Jesus' Claim to Divinity Leaves You With Only Three Options. Either:

- He was a liar
- He was a lunatic
- He was who He claimed to be!

That is the problem all other religions must answer and cannot. They all say Jesus was a great moral teacher, or, a great prophet. But, that is the one thing you *cannot* say; He has not left that alternative open to us—He did not intend to.

Shop, Compare, and Save

Buddha said, "I'm a teacher in search of truth,"

Jesus said, "I am the truth."

Confucius said, "I never claimed to be holy."

Jesus said, "Which one of you convicts Me of sin?"

Mohammed said, "Unless God covers me with a cloak of mercy I have no hope."

Jesus said, "I am the resurrection and the life. He who believes in Me, though he die, yet shall he live."

None of these other men ever claimed to be God. They all said God is this way, go this way; and Jesus said,

I am the way, the truth and the life, no man comes to the Father but by Me (John 14:6).

This is a True Story

I will never forget the story that one well-known evangelist shared on one of his radio programs. He was invited to an Islamic country to debate a Muslim scholar. When asked to present his passport to the customs' officer, the man asked, "For what purpose do you want to enter my country; what is your business?"

He answered, "I am a Christian evangelist. I have been invited here for a debate."

The man said, "Sir, I would like to ask you one question. What do you think of Mohammed?" The whole room became dead silent as all the other customs' officials turned to hear his answer.

He answered with a question, "Sir, I would like to ask you a question, 'Can a prophet lie?'"

The officer thought for a moment, and answered, "No, a prophet cannot lie."

The evangelist asked, "Mohammed was a prophet?"

Officer, "Yes."

Evangelist, "Mohammed said Jesus was a prophet?"

Officer, "Yes."

Evangelist, "Jesus said He was God. If Jesus was right, Mohammed was wrong. And, if Jesus was wrong, Mohammed was still wrong because Mohammed said Jesus was right!"

The officer stamped his passport and said, "You may go."

The Greatest Words Ever Spoken

If you are still not convinced of the deity of Christ, then you need to read His words yourself. Some of the most infamous people in history have been changed forever after reading His revelation known as, "The Sermon on the Mount." It's found in Matthew chapters 5-7 in the Bible.

Truly, no man has ever spoken with a greater perspective on eternity than Jesus did. No one has ever spoken such words of love, wisdom, integrity, compassion, or insight into the future before or since.

One sentence from the lips of Jesus would fix the world. These are the words of the Master Himself,

It is more blessed to give than to receive.

If we all lived by that divine truth, we would live in a perfect world. I challenge you to find anyone in all of history that can even begin to compare to Jesus.

If there is no God then life has no meaning, and the world is an inexplicable riddle. If the Bible is true, then love matters, life has meaning, and the history of the human race is satisfactorily explained.

The Great "I Am" Revealed

There are seven "I am" sayings of Jesus in the New Testament. Each one is a clear reference to Exodus 3:14 (written 1,500 years earlier) when God revealed His name to Moses,

I am, that I am, tell them I am hath sent you.

So, when Jesus said, "Before Abraham was I am," the Pharisees knew exactly what He meant, and they wanted to stone Him for claiming to be God (Jn. 8:58, 59 & 10:30, 31).

Jesus did not just *say* He was God—anyone can say that! Jesus said and *did* things that only God could say and do! For example, Jesus said,

"I am the light of the world." But, He did not just *say*, "I am the light of the world," He *said*, "I am the light of the world," and He gave sight to a man born blind! Jesus said,

"I am the bread of life," But, He did not just *say*, "I am the bread of life," He *said*, "I am the bread of life," and He fed five thousand people with a few fish and a couple of loaves of bread!

He said, "I am the resurrection and the life," and He called forth Lazarus from the dead!

Each of the "I am" sayings was accompanied by a miracle which in turn revealed attributes that belong to God alone. The one miracle that Jesus performed more than any other was giving sight to the blind. Compare that to what God said to Moses in Exodus 4:11,

And the LORD said to him, "Who has made man's mouth? Or who makes {him} dumb or deaf, or seeing or blind? Is it not I, the LORD?"

These three "I am," sayings show Jesus to be the Creator, the Sustainer, and the Redeemer of mankind.

Seeing is Believing

When you look at a skyscraper in a city like Chicago, it requires no "faith" on your part to *know* there was a designer and a builder. While it is true I have never seen this person, the building itself is *empirical proof* they exist! Jesus used the same argument in John 14:9-11,

> Jesus said to him, "Have I been with you so long, and yet you have not known Me, Philip? He who has seen Me has seen the Father; so how can you say, 'Show us the Father'? Do you not believe that I am in the Father, and the Father in Me? The words that I speak to you I do not speak on My own authority; but the Father who dwells in Me does the works. Believe Me that I am in the Father and the Father in Me, or else believe Me for the sake of the works themselves.

Jesus was speaking of the miracles He was performing to demonstrate His deity. Anyone can "say" they are God. But, only God can give sight to the blind, calm a storm, walk on water, cleanse a leper, predict the future with perfect accuracy, forgive sin, and raise the dead! Jesus did all that and much more.

If You Don't Believe in the Resurrection of Jesus then the Onus is on You to Produce a More Authoritative and Compelling Argument Than This One...

"Simon Greenleaf (1783-1853) was the famous Royal Professor of Law at Harvard University and succeeded Justice Joseph Story as the Dane Professor of Law in the same university, upon Story's death in 1846. H. W. H. Knott says of this great authority in jurisprudence: 'To the efforts of Story and Greenleaf is to be ascribed the rise of the Harvard Law School to its eminent position among the legal schools of the United States.'

"Greenleaf produced a famous work entitled *A Treatise on the Law of Evidence* which is still considered the greatest single authority on evidence in the entire literature of legal procedure.

"In 1846, while still Professor of Law at Harvard, Greenleaf wrote a volume entitled: *An Examination of the Testimony of the Four Evangelists by the Rules of Evidence Administered in the Courts of Justice*. In his classic work the author examines the value of the testimony of the apostles to the resurrection of Christ. The following are this brilliant jurist's critical observations."

> The great truths which the apostles declared were that Christ had risen from the dead, and that only through repentance from sin and faith in Him, could men hope for salvation. This doctrine they asserted with one voice, everywhere, not only under the greatest discouragements, but in the face of the most appalling errors that can be presented to the mind of man.
>
> Their master had recently perished as a malefactor, by the sentence of a public tribunal. His religion sought to overthrow the religions of the whole world. The laws of every country were against the teachings of His disciples. The interests and passions of all the rulers and great men in the world were against them. The fashion of the world was against them.
>
> Propagating this new faith, even in the most inoffensive and peaceful manner, they could expect nothing but contempt, opposition, reviling's, bitter persecutions, stripes, imprisonments, torments, and cruel deaths.
>
> Yet this faith they zealously did propagate; and all these miseries they endured undismayed, nay, rejoicing. As one after another was put to a miserable death, the survivors only prosecuted their work with increased vigor and resolution. The annals of military warfare afford scarcely an example of the like heroic constancy, patience, and unblenching courage.
>
> They had every possible motive to review carefully the grounds of their faith, and the evidences of the great facts and truths which they asserted; and these motives were pressed upon their attention with the most melancholy and terrific frequency. It was therefore impossible that they could have persisted in affirming the truths they have narrated, had not Jesus actually risen from the dead. [1]

Don't Miss this Closing Thought

It was 2,000 years ago when the Roman Empire ruled the world with an iron fist. They won all their arguments by killing their enemies.

It is a well-established, historical fact that the Roman Empire killed Christians by feeding them to lions. Today we have the incredible perspective of being able to look back over 2,000 years of recorded history, and what do we see?

There are more Christians alive at this moment than the total number of people that made up the Roman Empire over its entire 500 year history, and the lions and the tigers are on the endangered species list! We're not afraid of lions, bring `em on!

With more than two billion followers right now, Jesus Christ is the most famous person in history!

Chapter Three

There Is No Excuse
for Unbelief

"I'm not a sinner. I'm a good person. I've never murdered anyone. Why do I need a savior?" You may be a good person, but by whose standard?

If God compared you to Adolph Hitler or Joseph Stalin, you would probably compare very favorably. But, what if He compared you to Jesus Christ?

The Ten Commandments are God's perfect moral standard, and by that standard, no one is "good." Consider what each commandment says and means.

The First Commandment:
You Shall Have No Other Gods Before Me

Stated positively, this means you shall "love the LORD your God with all your heart, mind, soul, and strength." So, what does it mean to love God with all your heart? Jesus said, "If you love Me you will keep My commands." But, God is perfect. Followed through to its logical conclusion, that would require perfect obedience, which is another way of saying sinless perfection. No mere man has ever loved God like that.

If the greatest commandment is to love God with all your heart, then the greatest sin cannot be murder. The greatest sin must be not to love the God who created you more than the things He created. That brings us to the next command.

The Second Commandment:
Thou Shalt Not Make Unto Thee Any Graven Images

The first commandment tells us Who to worship; the second commandment tells us how–in spirit and in truth. That is, by faith and according to His Word–the Bible. Noted author Ray Comfort explains just what that means for us:

"You are not to make a god with your hands or with your mind. I have people tell me that my god is a god of love; he would never send anyone to hell. I agree with them. Their god would never send anyone to hell, because their god doesn't exist. He's a god made in their own image.

"The Bible says, 'God is a consuming fire.' He has a passion for justice, holiness, righteousness and truth. He will by no means clear the guilty, but will hold every man accountable for every idle word he speaks."

Whatever you love most, that is your god. If it's not the true and living God, you are guilty of breaking this commandment—you are an idol worshipper.

The Third Commandment:
You Shall Not Take the Name of the Lord In Vain

When a man gets angry enough he will often take the name God or the name Jesus Christ and use it to curse. Blasphemy is defined as the act of speaking sacrilegiously about God or sacred things.

The ancient Jews were so fearful of breaking this command they dared not even *speak* the most holy name of God because the commandment goes on to say, "the LORD will not leave him unpunished who takes His name in vain." Have you ever committed the sin of blasphemy?

The Fourth Commandment:
Remember the Sabbath to Keep It Holy

The idea here is to take one day out of seven, and to set aside all your worldly amusements, and your effort to better your position in this world, and rest. And in that rest, acknowledge the God who created you, the God who sustains you, and the God who purchased your salvation with His own blood (Acts 20:28).

Ultimately, our rest is in the finished work of Christ on the cross. When Jesus died on the cross His last words were, "It is finished." His words could be just as accurately translated, "Paid in full." There is nothing you can add or take away from the perfect sacrifice of Christ on the cross.

The Bible teaches that we are saved (from the guilt, the power, and the penalty of sin) by grace alone, through faith alone, through Christ alone—plus, nothing!

Salvation is God's free gift to all who truly repent and believe that Jesus died for our sin and rose again. Christ is not just our Savior, He *is* our salvation. A new spiritual life is the effect of salvation, never the cause of it.

Christianity is more than a religion, it's a revelation. And once you've experienced the revelation, you are born into a personal love relationship with God through His Son, the Lord Jesus Christ.

The Fifth Commandment:
Honor Your Father and Your Mother

Abraham Lincoln once said, "The strength of a nation lies in the homes of its people. As go the families, so goes the nation."

Our world is in trouble because our families are in trouble. Many fathers have failed to take the role of spiritual leaders in their homes, and train their children to love God and to love their neighbors as themselves. Conversely, many children have rebelled against parents who did model the love of God.

The parent–child relationship is sacred because it began in the mind of God. The parents entrusted with the message of salvation are to raise godly offspring who will in turn pass the message of salvation to their children and so on and so forth.

To rebel against one's parents was a capital offense in the Old Testament, since to do so was to rebel against God's ordained hierarchy of authority. God is a God of law and order. We see this in all of creation. Without law and order there is rebellion and chaos.

Adolph Hitler was one of the most notorious mass murderers in history

The Sixth Commandment:
Thou Shalt Not Murder

Jesus said, "You have heard that it was said, 'You shall not murder', but I say to you that whoever is angry with his brother (or calls him empty headed or a fool) will be in danger of judgment and the fires of hell" (Matthew 5:21, 22).

The physical act of murder begins as a spiritual act in the heart as unforgiveness or hatred. Since we have all sinned, none of us has the right not to forgive. Jesus taught that we are to forgive even as we have been forgiven (Matthew 6:14, 15). God alone has jurisdiction to judge the sins of men righteously. In Hebrews 10:30 God says, "Vengeance is Mine. I will repay."

The number one psychological condition of people who are put into mental institutions is anger. The anger is based on unforgiveness.

When you choose not to forgive someone, you can become bitter, angry, and depressed. The prescription for a sound mind and great relationships is found in Romans 13:8,

> Owe no one anything except to love one another, for he who loves another has fulfilled the law.

The Seventh Commandment:
Thou Shalt Not Commit Adultery

The first institution God ordained in the book of Genesis was marriage, then the family. The act of marriage between a husband and wife is sacred because it originated in the mind of God!

Our Creator could have populated the earth any way He wanted to. Intimacy with one's marital partner is not only a gift from God, but typifies our relationship to Him. It also testifies to the fact that we are "Made in His image."

- First, we are like God in that a husband and a wife have the ability to create life.
- Second, the act of marriage speaks of intimate love and oneness.
- Third, we are to have this relationship with no one else.

Jesus raised the bar even higher when He said,

> You have heard that it was said, "You shall not commit adultery," but I say to you that whoever looks at a woman to lust after her has committed adultery already, in his heart (Matthew 5:28).

This is the Most Politically Incorrect Thing You Can Say to Another Human Being, but it's Also the Most Loving.

I like what Ray Comfort said, "To tell a man he's a sinner without telling him what sin is, is like telling a man he's under arrest without telling him what he's charged with."

In John 16:8, we learn that the Holy Spirit's ministry is to "convict the world of sin, righteousness, and judgment." The word *convict* in the original Greek literally means:

- To show or prove one of wrong

- To expose the hidden things

- To correct or chastise in a *moral* sense

Walking a person gently and lovingly through the Ten Commandments, and explaining the spiritual application of each one, showing how all of us have broken God's law in thought, word, and deed, is absolutely, positively the most convicting, compelling, personal, embarrassing, and most loving things you can say to another human being. Why? Because it is sin that separates us from God (Isa. 59:2), and it is sin that Jesus came to save us from (Matt. 1:21). We have all broken God's law, and everyone, whether they will admit or not, knows it's true!

Watch what happens when you tell a man that the seventh commandment condemns looking at women with lust or viewing pornography. I have seen many men break–out in a cold sweat, others begin to shake, and still others literally break down in tears after seeing themselves in the mirror of God's law. Spiritual truth transends the human intellect, and speaks to the heart!

You are Not What You Think You Are, But What You Think You Are

Your mind is not a garbage dump; it's a temple (1 Cor. 2:16, 3:17). God wants you to set your mind on things that are pure and holy. Why? Good deeds and bad begin in the mind as a thought. The great commandment is to love God with all our heart, *mind*, soul, and strength. That is why God wants you to have a sanctified imagination.

Your behavior (good or bad) is based on what you have allowed yourself to think and believe. As the old saying goes,

> Sow a thought, reap an action. Sow an action, reap a habit. Sow a habit, reap a character. Sow a character, reap a destiny.

The Devastating Effects of Adultery

"Research shows that infidelity causes insecurity, anger, confusion and mistrust; it often leads to depression and divorce. Statistics show that children from broken homes are far more likely to get involved in drug and alcohol abuse. Fatherless children are twice as likely to drop out of school and suffer from emotional and behavioral problems. They are more likely to engage in immoral behavior, criminal activity and are five times more likely to live in poverty."

God intended children to be raised by a father and a mother who would be faithful to Him, and to each other. Love begins in the home, and children are gifts from God (Ps. 127 & 128).

God gave us these laws not to rob us, but to protect us from robbing ourselves. Blessings follow those who follow God's Word. In John 10:10 Jesus said,

> I came that they might have life and have it more abundantly.

You Will Not Find a Higher Moral Code in Any Religion, Philosophy, or System of Thought

The doctrine of marital fidelity is a foreign concept to all man-made religions. The Judeo-Christian worldview alone teaches that human sexuality is sacred (because it began in the mind of God), and is exclusive. In Genesis 2:24 God said,

> Therefore a man shall leave his father and mother and be joined to his wife, and the two shall become one flesh.

Then, in Genesis 39:9 (500 years before God gave Moses the Ten Commandments), we find Joseph resisting the advances of his boss' wife by saying,

> There is no one greater in this house than I, nor has he kept back anything from me but you, because you are his wife. How then can I do this great wickedness, and sin against God?

How could Joseph have such a deep conviction 500 years before Mt. Sinai? Romans 2:15 provides the answer,

The law is written on every man's heart.

In other words, every man from the beginning of time until the end of the world, whether or not he has ever heard of Jesus or even seen a Bible, knows instinctively that it is wrong to murder, to steal, to lie, and it's wrong to have another man's wife! There is no other way to account for this fact other than to acknowledge that our Creator placed His moral law in every human heart.

Christianity Outshines All Man-Made Religions

It was 1,500 B.C. when God gave Moses the Ten Commandments. At the time, pagan religions included sexual immorality as a form of worship to their gods. Both the Canaanites and the Babylonians included temple prostitution in their worship of Baal. The Greeks and Romans also had their own versions of "sanctified prostitution."

Islam: The Koran says a Muslim man may have 4 wives and numerous concubines. Mohammed, the founder of Islam, had 11 wives. Joseph Smith, the founder of Mormonism had 33 wives!

"Nature" itself teaches that the doctrine of polygamy cannot be divinely inspired since the ratio of men to women in the world is 1 to 1. If there were 10 women to every man in the world this doctrine might not be so obviously false. It's also grossly unfair to women. Islamic law does not allow a woman to have four husbands. I don't wonder why.

Hinduism: In India, the devadasi (day-vah-dah-see) system is the Hindu practice of young girls engaging in temple prostitution. Girls as young as 11-12 are told they are "dedicating" themselves to Hindu gods! This practice goes back more than 5,000 years.

Children from a lower social status (called a lower "caste") are often forced by parents to begin a life of prostitution. This horrific sin is exacerbated by social and economic pressure.

Ironically (and hypocritically) high caste Hindu priests will not eat from or even touch the cup or bowl of a lower caste Hindu, but they will have sexual intercourse with them!

Buddhism: This religion has no explicit sexual code. Having no code, by default, is a code. Many Buddhist monks have expressed the opinion that engaging in prostitution purely for helping others can be a source of karmic merit. One of the "helps" they provide is by making offerings and gifts to Buddhist temples. That is one reason the Buddhist hierarchy is silent on prostitution, and one reason many temples are so lavish.

Christianity: In Deuteronomy 23:17-18 the Bible says, "There shall be no ritual harlot of the daughters of Israel, or a perverted one of the sons of Israel. You shall not bring the wages of a harlot or the price of a dog to the house of the Lord your God for any vowed offering, for both of these are an abomination to the Lord your God."

Faithfulness to one's marital partner in thought, word, and deed, and equality for women and children clearly sets Christianity apart from all man-made religions. What mortal man would make up a law against lust (as Jesus did), and who but God could enforce it?

The Eighth Commandment:
Thou Shalt Not Steal

The level of corruption that goes on behind closed doors in this age of technology is unfathomable to the average person. Financial firms who cook-the-books have caused many families to lose their life savings by investing in these fraudulent companies. One man recently made off (almost) with some 50 billion dollars in the largest Ponzi scheme on record, and that's just the tip of the iceberg. The large investment banks do it every day!

On the other end of the spectrum, retail theft is the number one crime in America—it's measured in terms of billions of dollars annually. Theft ranges from children taking candy bars to government officials and corporate executives stealing hundreds of billions of dollars. Stealing is the primary reason so many nations are on the verge of bankruptcy.

Stealing affects everybody. Do you know who pays for all this? You and I do, in the form of higher taxes and higher prices for everything. Sin is expensive.

Do you know how much you have to steal to be a thief? *Anything!* It's not the value of the thing, it's the principle of the thing. If you cheat someone out of a penny you have violated God's law. Proverbs 11:1 says,

> Dishonest scales are an abomination to the Lord, but a just weight is His delight.

The Ninth Commandment: Thou Shalt Not Lie

How many lies do you have to tell to be a liar? The same number of people you have to murder to be a murderer—just one. What is the cost of lying? Our political and judicial systems have been sabotaged by the philosophy that the best liar wins—but not for long. Proverbs 21:6 says,

> The getting of treasures by a lying tongue is the fleeting fantasy of those who seek death.

Do you realize what would happen if everyone stopped lying and everyone stopped stealing tomorrow? Think about it. There would be more than enough resources to provide safe, affordable housing, fresh food, and clean water for everyone.

Billions of dollars would be available for humanitarian aid. Nations around the world would no longer be bankrupt, and war would cease (war is based on lying, stealing and coveting). Many prisons would close. Frivolous lawsuits would end. Jesus said,

> You shall know the truth and the truth shall make you free.

The Tenth Commandment:
Thou Shalt Not Covet

Stated positively, this means: learn to be content with what you can earn with your own hands and your own mind.

We are commanded not to desire what belongs to our neighbor, including his house, his wife, his car, his title, his position, or his bank account.

Many Americans are in bondage to the idol of materialism. The average household is nearly $12,000 in debt to their credit cards, or better, 'covet' cards. In many cases, we buy things we don't need with money we don't have, to impress people we don't even like. If you don't have the money for it, you can't afford it. Covetousness is actually the essence of all sin.

The first sin in the universe was committed when Lucifer said, "I will exalt myself above the throne of God." He coveted the glory that belongs to God alone.

The first sin on earth was committed when Adam and Eve ate the forbidden fruit. They wanted to be like God knowing good and evil. And, it was covetousness that caused the Pharisees to arrange for the murder of Jesus because they were envious of His ministry. According to Col. 3:15, covetousness is idolatry. Idolatry is spiritual adultery, an abomination to God.

The Christian Life Isn't Difficult—It's Impossible.
Nobody Could Live Up to this Standard!

The Bible says *all* men have sinned, that is why all men die (Rom.3:23). Simply stated, it's because we have broken God's law (sinned) that we need His grace. Grace is God's unmerited favor.

In the Old Testament, an animal was offered as a sacrifice for sin. The animal had to be perfect, that is, without spot or blemish. It could not be blind or lame. This outer perfection was symbolic. God can only accept a perfect sacrifice, which means, sinless perfection!

The spot (if the sacrifice had one) was inherited, and the blemish was acquired. This speaks of the fact that we are sinners by nature, and we are sinners by choice.

When the Virgin Mary was impregnated, not by the seed of man but by the Spirit of God, what was begotten nine months later was God in a human body. Because Jesus was not born of the seed of man, He had no inherited sin (spot). And, because He kept the Law perfectly, He had no acquired sin (blemish). That is why the Bible refers to Jesus as "The Lamb of God without spot or blemish."

Since the penalty for sin is death, in order for a savior to save you, he would have to be sinless and die for you. That is precisely what Jesus did on the cross. His death satisfied the righteous penalty for breaking God's moral law. This allows God to legally and morally forgive repent sinners without compromising His justice. This makes perfect sense. Justice and mercy have kissed (Ps. 85:10). Redemption by the blood sacrifice of Jesus Christ is the whole point of the Bible from cover to cover; also known as God's grace, this is what makes Christianity utterly unique!

How Does Christ's Death Apply?

While living in the Chicago area, I became engaged to the young lady who is now my wife, Susan. While it was the Lord's idea in the first place, I still wanted the blessing of my future in-laws who lived in Nevada.

My fiancée flew out a few weeks before I did. When I arrived, they were expecting me. I knocked on the door, and without hesitation they invited me in. Later that night we had a wonderful dinner together. A few hours later, I was escorted to my own, private bedroom, and was told, "Make yourself at home."

The next day, my future mother-in-law said, "You're going to need to get around, so here's the key to the car!"

Can you imagine what might have happened if I, a perfect stranger, had knocked on the wrong door and asked for food, a place to stay for the night, the keys to their car, and their daughter's hand in marriage? The sandwich might have been achievable, but the rest would have been out of the question!

I was accepted and treated like a son because I knocked on the right door. In John chapter 10 Jesus said,

> I am the door.

I came in the right name, which in this case was "Susan." In Acts chapter 4, speaking of the name of Jesus, we read,

> There is no other name under heaven by which we must be saved.

I came to the right door, I came in the right name, and I came with the right motive, which was love. In 1 John 4:19, the Bible says,

> We love Him because He first loved us.

Marriage is a covenant, and the rings are the symbols of that covenant. But, with God we have something infinitely greater; we have a blood covenant through Jesus Christ.

Now any inheritance that belongs to my wife also belongs to me, and my inheritance also belongs to her. In exactly the same way, the inheritance of eternal life that Jesus won on the cross now belongs to all who have a personal, love relationship with Him. That is how it works in the kingdom of God.

> Therefore having been justified by faith, we have peace with God through our Lord Jesus Christ, through whom also we have obtained our introduction by faith into this grace in which we stand; and we exult in hope of the glory of God (Rom. 5:1, 2).

In the same way, when you come to God the Father in the name of His Son, Jesus, you are "accepted in the beloved" (Eph.1:6). We are called "children of God" (Phil. 2:15). We become "co-heirs with Christ" (Rom. 8:16, 17). He is our heavenly Bridegroom and the Church is His bride.

A Closing Story

I met a man recently and asked him what he did for a living. He said, "I'm a Professor of Philosophy and Comparative Religion at the local college." I asked, "Are you an atheist?" He said, "Yes. What do you do?" I said, "I write Christian books!"

I asked, "So, you believe that nobody, plus nothing equals everything?" His answer was profound. He said, "What?" An hour-and-a-half later, after *gently* walking him through God's three arguments, he could not refute a thing I said! My goal however, was not to win an argument; I was trying to win his heart.

In a legitimate debate, Charles Darwin (or anyone else for that matter) is no match for Jesus Christ. When you're right *about* God, and you're right *with* God, you never have to be intimidated by the world, the flesh, or the devil himself—and it's okay to get excited about Jesus!

Chapter Four

How Can One God Be a Trinity?

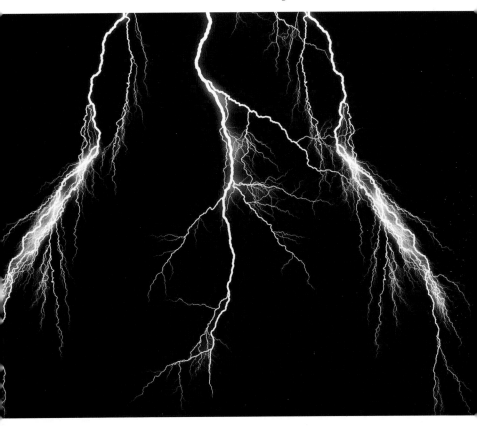

Is the Trinity a blatant contradiction? Do Christians really worship three gods, as the skeptics claim? If the Trinity is true, then Christianity alone is correct about the nature of God.

Can the Trinity be demonstrated? The fact is, our world is filled with tri-unities. Here are some fascinating examples of the trinity in nature:

Einstein's Theory of Relativity revealed the fact that life as we know it consists of three things: time, space, and matter (which is energy). This is a trinity of trinities.

Time: Time is a trinity—the past, the present, and the future. The past is not the present, the present is not the future, and the future is not the past. One is not the other, all are part of the same, none can exist without the other, and yet each one is distinct!

Space: We live in a three-dimensional world—height, width, and depth. Height is not width, width is not depth, and depth is not height. One is not the other, all are part of the same, none can exist without the other, and yet each one is distinct!

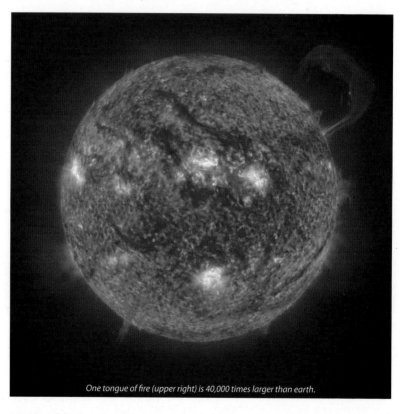

One tongue of fire (upper right) is 40,000 times larger than earth.

Matter: Matter is made up of atoms, and atoms consist of three basic components: protons, neutrons, and electrons. A proton is not a neutron, a neutron is not an electron, and an electron is not a proton.

One is not the other, all are part of the same, none can exist without the other (being a complete atom), and yet each one is distinct!

Two thousand years after the New Testament was written, we still cannot see an atom. Yet in Hebrews 11:3 the Bible says,

> By faith we understand that the worlds were prepared by the word of God, so that what is seen was not made out of things which are visible.

That verse did not make any sense until the discovery of the atom. Interesting too is the fact that protons are positively charged and electrons are negatively charged. Having all the positively charged protons so extremely close together, should result in a tremendous repulsive force, like trying to hold two magnets together. Science has yet to discover what holds atoms together. But in Colossians 1:17, the Bible says,

> And… and in Him (Jesus) all things hold together.

Made in the Image of God
Man is Body, Soul, and Spirit

I Thessalonians 5:23 says,

> Now may the God of peace Himself sanctify you entirely; and may your spirit and soul and body be preserved complete, without blame at the coming of our Lord Jesus Christ.

According to this verse, you have a triune nature consisting of a body, a soul, and a spirit. In the original Greek language of the New Testament:

- The word for body is *soma*,
- The word for soul is *psuche*,
- The word for spirit is *pneuma*.

One is not the other, all are part of the same, none can exist without the other, and yet each one is distinct!

The human mind: Scientists tell us that the human brain is the most complex thing in the universe (that we know of). The brain houses the mind, and the mind is a trinity—the mind (intellect), the will, and the emotions.

Your mind is not the same as your emotions. Your emotions are not the same as your will, and your will is not the same as your intellect. One is not the other, all are part of the same, none can exist without the other, and yet each one is distinct!

There are many more examples that can be offered for the triune nature of the world around us. A good case can be made for the triune nature of earth, wind, fire, water, light, and many more. Even the earth is the third planet from the sun!

Water

One molecule of water is made up of three atoms—two hydrogen and one oxygen. Interestingly, if you separate the hydrogen from the oxygen, pure hydrogen is highly flammable and pure oxygen is also highly flammable. But, if you put the two together in a 2 to 1 ratio, you have a third substance which you can use to extinguish a fire! Can you rationally understand that?

Have you ever had eggs for breakfast? One egg consists of the shell, the white, and the yolk. Were you eating three eggs?

I have just demonstrated mathematically and scientifically that the Trinity is not an unfathomable, illogical, irrational contradiction. There are tri-unities all around us which reflect the triune nature of our Creator.

How a mortal man who has never seen God and cannot even begin to fathom His eternal nature, can insist that God cannot be triune is more of a mystery than the Trinity itself.

If you are still adamant that God cannot be a Trinity, I'll ask you the same question God asked Job (in Job chapter 38) when he was questioning God:

> Who is this who darkens counsel by words without knowledge? Now prepare yourself like a man; I will question you, and you shall answer Me. Where were you when I laid the foundations of the earth? Tell Me, if you have understanding.

I am indebted to Dr. Henry Morris and the late Adrian Rogers for these excellent insights on the Trinity.

Chapter Five

Evolution Is Not Science
It's Monkey Mythology

If man evolved from monkeys, why do we still have monkeys?

If evolution is a proven scientific fact, why are so many of the world's leading scientists speaking out against the so-called "evidence" for evolution? Some of the finest minds in the world have called it "The greatest hoax in history," and "Monkey Mythology." Keep reading and you will see why.

There is now a list of more than 700 PhD scientists who have signed a petition stating that they are dissenters of Darwin's theory. This is the website: www.dissentfromdarwin.org.

If there are 700 honest scientists who are not afraid to speak out publicly, that means there are many more who also disagree with evolution but are afraid to state their views publicly for fear of losing their jobs. Ben Stein, a secular researcher, documented this fact well in his DVD film documentary, *Expelled*. This exposed the censorship,

bias, and outright suppression of the mountains of evidence for intelligent design. I highly recommend this excellent DVD.

Macro-evolution (one species becoming another) has never been observed in a laboratory (or anywhere else for that matter)! Neither are there any fossils that offer any evidence that evolution ever occurred. Read what Darwin himself admitted concerning his theory of evolution and the Fossil Record.

Charles Darwin Rightly Rejects His Own Theory

Firstly, why, if species have descended from other species by insensibly fine gradations, do we not everywhere see innumerable transitional forms? Why is not all nature in confusion instead of the species being, as we see them, well defined? [1]

According to this theory, innumerable transitional forms must have existed; why do we not find them embedded in countless numbers in the crust of the earth?" [2]

Lastly, looking not to any one time, but to all time, if the theory is true, numberless intermediate varieties, linking closely together all the species of the same group, must assuredly have existed. [3]

Why then is not every geological formation and every stratum full of such intermediate links? [4]

He who rejects this view of the imperfection of the geological record will rightly reject the whole theory. [5]

How very ironic it is that Darwin posed these questions himself. This idea is so important it merits repeating. In Darwin's own words, if his theory of evolution were true, we would discover fossils all over the world showing intermediate stages of biological development. If we do not, then his theory is incorrect.

What Does the Fossil Record Show?

"Author Luther Sunderland interviewed five respected museum officials, recognized authorities in their individual fields of study, including representatives from the American Museum, the Field Museum of Natural History in Chicago, and the British Museum of Natural History. None of the five officials were able to offer a single example of a transitional series of fossilized organisms that document the transformation of one kind of plant or animal into another.

"Among the five respected museum officials, Sunderland interviewed Dr. Colin Patterson, Senior Paleontologist at the British Museum and editor of a prestigious scientific journal. Patterson is a well-known expert having an intimate knowledge of the fossil record. He was unable to give a single example of macro-evolutionary transition.

"Patterson wrote a book for the British Museum of Natural History entitled, *Evolution*. When asked why he had not included a single photograph of a transitional fossil in his book, Patterson responded:

"I fully agree with your comments on the lack of direct illustration of evolutionary transitions in my book. If I knew of any I would certainly have included them. Yet Gould and the American Museum people are hard to contradict when they say there are no transitional fossils. As a paleontologist myself, I am much occupied with the philosophical problems of identifying ancestral forms in the fossil record. You say that I should at least "show a photo of the fossil from which each type of organism was derived." I will lay it on the line: there is not one such fossil for which one could make a watertight argument.

"Ask an evolutionary college professor to explain how evolution can be called science in light of the following facts: Our museums now contain hundreds of millions of fossil specimens (40 million are contained in the Smithsonian Natural History Museum alone). If Darwin's theory were true, we should see tens of millions of unquestionably transitional forms. We see none.

"In fact, based on standard mathematical models, we would see far more transitional forms in the fossil record than complete specimens. However, we see none, not one true transitional specimen has ever been found. You would also expect to see transitional forms walking around today. But no, all we see are fully formed animals. Dogs are dogs, cats are cats, fish are fish, and birds are birds.

"In Darwin's day (the mid-1800s), paleontology was a new branch of science. Today, 150 years later, the fossil record proves Darwin's theory was wrong. Let me state it another way, the fossil record utterly fails to confirm Darwin's theory." [6]

What About Mutations?

It is amazing how far men will go to deny the existence of God. Many false claims are made by evolutionists. There appears to be no end to their shell game with words and "discoveries."

Many so called "scientists" claim that mutations within species prove evolution to be true. What they don't tell you is, mutations are extremely rare occurrences and are mistakes, with negative, not positive effects on cells!

"The fact is mutations are permanent changes in the DNA cell. They are mistakes not corrections. Mutations are the basis for genetic disorders and disease. They result in defective protein molecules that don't work properly.

"It's easy to make mutations that create "nonsense" sentences. Can you make mutations that maintain or change the meaning of the sentence without creating such nonsense? Scientists claim mutations

"If anything now exists either something is eternal, or no one, plus nothing equals everything." —Walter Martin

are responsible for the evolving of simple cells into more complex ones.

"Something I find amusing is the fact that scientists are working fervently to create life from non-living matter in a laboratory in an attempt to prove evolution. If they ever do succeed, they would only prove that it required intelligence not random chance to make it happen!

"Another thing they conveniently fail to mention is the fact that no scientist at any time has ever observed one species evolving into another species, a fish turning into a bird for example.

"Charles Darwin himself admitted that if his "theory" of evolution were true, the fossil record would either prove or disprove his hypothesis. That was more than 150 years ago. Literally millions of fossils have been discovered since that time and to this day, not one single fossil has ever been discovered showing one species developing into another species. In fact, the fossil record shows just the opposite. Birds have always been birds and fish have always been fish." [7]

Darwin was Wrong Again

In 1859 Charles Darwin mistakenly believed cells were simple and evolved by chance. Today we know cells are extremely complex. One DNA cell contains enough coded information to fill a 1,000 volume encyclopedia set, each with 500 pages!

The second law of thermodynamics demonstrates that the universe is breaking down—becoming simpler—not more complex. No fossils of intermediate life forms have ever been found to prove evolution is true.

Atheists Aren't Born—They Evolve

A study was done a while back into all the famous atheists of history, Jean Paul Sartre, Camus, Friedrich Nietzsche, Sigmund Freud, Karl Marx, Madalyn Murray O'Hair, and every single one of them had something in common. They either lost their father when they were young, their father abandoned their family, or they had a terrible relationship with their father. That is very interesting because often these doubts aren't really driven by intellectual questions; they are being driven by an emotional issue that really blocks them from wanting to relate to a heavenly father because they feel so abandoned, or cheated, or hurt by their earthly father. —Lee Strobel

What is the Real Motive Behind Atheism?

The famous atheist Aldous Huxley speaks for all atheists (whether they like it or not) in this priceless quote:

I had motives for not wanting the world to have meaning; consequently assumed it had none, and was able without any difficulty to find satisfying reasons for this assumption … The philosopher who finds no meaning in the world is not concerned exclusively with a problem of pure metaphysics; he is also concerned to prove there is no valid reason why he personally should not do as he wants to do. For myself, as no doubt for most of my contemporaries, the philosophy of meaninglessness was essentially an instrument of liberation. The liberation we desired was simultaneously liberation from a certain political and economic system, and liberation from a certain system of morality. We objected to the morality because it interfered with our sexual freedom.

Atheism is actually a crutch for those who cannot bear the thought of identifying themselves with our great God and Savior Jesus Christ and admitting they *are* sinners.

If evolution is true, then life has no meaning, and the world is an inexplicable riddle. If the Bible is true, then love matters, life has meaning, and the origin of the human race is satisfactorily explained.

The Russians Are Coming!

It was April 12, 1961, when the Russians sent the first, manned rocket into space. Yuri Gagarin ascended 188 miles, circled the earth and returned safely. Shortly thereafter, the atheistic Russian government held a press conference. They proudly announced to the world that their man had gone up to the heavens, looked around for God and did not see Him. The obvious implication was they now had a first-hand, eye-witness account that God did not exist.

Well, had Yuri gone just one foot farther it would have been a different story. If he just would have stepped outside of his little space craft and shut the door behind him, in about three minutes he would have seen God!

Atheism, pure and simple, is based on emotions, not the intellect. As Josh McDowell has admitted,

> I didn't want to believe in a heavenly father because I hated my own father—until I realized how much God loved me.

Could this be the Missing Link?

Here's a good one from W.A. Criswell,

> Once I was a tadpole beginning to begin. Then I was a frog with my tail tucked in. Then I was a monkey in a banana tree. Now I'm a professor with a PhD.

This quote by G.K. Chesterton is both amusing and accurate,

> The evolutionist seems to know everything about the missing link except the fact that it is missing!

A Closing Thought

The real reason the atheist can't find God
is the same reason a bank robber can't find a policeman!

How to Cultivate a Relationship with God

I n the preamble to the Ten Commandments, God introduces Himself to the world by revealing His most holy and proper name. He speaks in Exodus 20:1:

> Then God spoke all these words, saying, "I am the LORD your God, who brought you out of the land of Egypt, out of the house of slavery. You shall have no other gods before Me."

In Hebrew, the word translated "LORD" in the English Bible is actually a name rather than a title. It consists of four consonants, YHWH (pronounced yood hay vav hay), and no vowels. It represents the most holy and proper name of God.

While we don't know the exact pronunciation, we know what this name means. The name YHWH literally means, "The Eternal, Self-Existent One." In other words, He's the God who is, the God who was, and the God who always will be, from eternity past, to eternity future, without beginning, and without end. As the Eternal, Self-

Existent One, He is not dependent on anything outside of Himself to exist.

God is omnipotent, omniscient, and omnipresent. He is the Creator, the Sustainer, and the Redeemer of mankind. God is a person and you can know Him. In John 17:3-4, Jesus prayed,

> And this is eternal life, that they may know You, the only true God, and Jesus Christ whom You have sent.

Consider the wealth of liberating knowledge found in this seemingly insignificant, little, personal pronoun "I" in "I am the Lord." God's Word dispels the false doctrines of:

- Atheism: The idea that there is no God.

- Agnosticism: The idea that man is incapable of knowing if God exists. No one had to convince the people who were at Mt. Sinai that God exists. The sun, moon, and stars still do.

- Polytheism: The doctrine of many gods. There are some religions that believe in millions of gods.

- Pantheism: The "New Age" (which is really not new at all) belief that God is all, and all is God.

What if We All Obeyed this Command?

When Jesus was asked, "What is the greatest commandment in the law?" His answer is found in Matthew 22:37-39,

"'You shall love the Lord your God with all your heart, with all your soul, and with all your mind.' This is the first and great commandment. And the second is like it: 'You shall love your neighbor as yourself.'"

Here Jesus takes the Ten Commandments, distills them down to two, and states them positively. The first four teach us how to love God, and the next six teach us how to love our neighbor.

God's will for you is to love Him supremely, and to love your neighbor as yourself. Life is all about loving relationships. If you had all the money in the world but no one to share it with, what fun would that be?

Romans chapter 13 speaks of the Ten Commandments as the law of love, and James chapter 2 calls them the "perfect law of liberty."

Imagine what would happen if everyone loved God with all of their hearts and loved their neighbors as themselves? It's so simple and yet so profound.

Look back at the Ten Commandments, one at a time, and ask yourself, "What would happen if everyone obeyed this commandment?"

The Treasure Map to Eternal Life

What you are about to read is true and, it's exclusive to Christianity. This is the most amazing, wonderful, life-changing truth you could ever know.

As we have already mentioned, God is a person (as opposed to an obscure power or an impersonal force), and you can *know* Him.

You will not find this promise in any other so-called religion. Christianity is a revelation. And, once you've had the revelation, you are led into a personal, love relationship with God. This is all made possible through His Son—the Lord Jesus Christ, and by the power of His Spirit.

Here is how to cultivate a relationship with God according to His Word, beginning in Deuteronomy 4:29,

> But from there you will seek the LORD your God, and you will find {Him} if you search for Him with all your heart and all your soul.

And this from Proverbs 2:1-5,

> My son, if you will receive my sayings, and treasure my commandments within you, make your ear attentive to wisdom, incline your heart to understanding; for if you cry for discernment, lift your voice for understanding; if you seek her as silver, and search for her as for hidden treasures; then you will discern the fear of the LORD, and discover the knowledge of God.

Now Matthew 7:7-8,

> Ask, and it shall be given to you; seek, and you shall find; knock, and it shall be opened to you. For everyone who asks receives, and he who seeks finds, and to him who knocks it shall be opened.

Now consider James 4:8,

> Draw near to God and He will draw near to you.

And finally, in Revelation 3:20, God turns the table around and now He is pursuing you! These are the words of Jesus,

> Behold, I stand at the door and knock; if anyone hears My voice and opens the door, I will come in to him, and will dine with him, and he with Me.

How do you open the door of your heart? In Matthew 4:17, the Bible says,

> From that time Jesus began to preach and to say, "Repent, for the kingdom of heaven is at hand."

Repent means to change your mind, turn around, and go the other way. Stop ignoring God and living as if He did not exist!

We are not talking about living a life of guilt and remorse; it's just the opposite. We all fall short every day. Asking for forgiveness is not a burden; it's liberating. Having a clear conscience is priceless.

Developing and maintaining intimacy with God means keeping short accounts with Him, and with everybody else. Repentance is not a one-time event; it's a lifestyle.

Asking for forgiveness from God and then forgiving those who have hurt you is one of the most freeing things you can do. In some cases, this may take time but, with God's help, you can be free from anger, bitterness, and unforgiveness.

Why Would Anyone Reject God?

The same reason Adam and Eve tried to cover their sin and shame with fig leaves and then hide behind a tree. People try to hide from God for the same reasons. Many people don't even want to think about it. I remember asking a waitress, "I'd like to get your opinion on something." She said,

"I'm sorry, I don't think." And she walked away!

This Is A True Story

I was sitting in a hotel watching the Discovery Channel when I saw a spectacular illustration. There was a teacher telling a sixth grade class they were going to do an experiment. The teacher said, "I'm going to hold up two cards. One has a long line and the other has a short line on it. We are going to bring in a student who is unaware of our experiment to see how he will answer. When I hold up the cards I want you to purposely answer incorrectly. I'll show you both cards and ask, "How many of you think this (holding out the longer line) is the shorter of the two lines? Raise your hands. Okay?" Everyone agreed.

The student was brought in and the test began. The teacher held up the two cards. With the long line in her right hand, and the short line in her left hand, she waved the long line and asked, "How many of you think this is the shorter of the two lines? Raise your hands." Everybody instantly raised their hands.

The child who was unaware of what was going on also raised his hand. They tried it again and again with different children, and each time the child raised his hand *knowing he was answering incorrectly!*

Do you understand the implications of this story? These kids were willing to throw their reason and their integrity out-the-window because they did not want to be perceived as different by the other kids! The same thing is true of most adults, too.

The Fear of Man is a Powerful Force

People are willing to turn their backs on what is true and right because of fear and pride. So, the emotions can over-rule the intellect.

When I got home, I related this story to my wife and children. I said to them,

> I would like to think if one of you were that experimental child, knowing everyone was answering incorrectly, you would have stood up and asked, "Does anybody have a ruler?" The right thing to do is stand up for what's right even if everyone else is wrong!

Are you like the child in this story? Will you go along with the crowd even if your eternal destiny is hanging in the balance? One of the most convicting verses in the Bible is when Jesus said,

> If you are ashamed of Me before men, I will be ashamed of you before My father in heaven. But if you acknowledge Me before men I will acknowledge you before My father in heaven.

Atheism is a Crutch

Many people cannot bear the thought of identifying themselves with Jesus Christ and admitting they are sinners. "After all, what would my friends think? They might call me a religious fanatic or a 'Jesus Freak.'"

This is why many people choose to ignore or deny God's existence. But, in Matthew 10, Jesus puts it in perspective,

> Do not fear man who can only kill the body. But fear God who can not only kill your body but cast your soul into hell.

Another reason people reject God is because they love the world and the things of the world more than the God who created it. That includes the passing "pleasure" of sin for a season. Sadly, many never take the time to think this through. All they can think about is the here and now. Their god is their belly!

The fact is—life is short and eternity is long. Sin is deadly, heaven and hell are real places, and Jesus is the same yesterday, today, and forever.

How short is time? Think about this. Psalm 90:12 says,

> Teach us to number our days that we might present to thee a heart of wisdom.

In other words, teach me to live in light of eternity, knowing that a day of reckoning is coming. Let's do what the psalmist said, let's number our days.

The average, American male lives to be 72 years old—that is 26,280 days. On average, he will spend eight of every 24 hours sleeping. That leaves him with 48 years, or 17,520 days. One third of the remaining time he will spend going to school and working. That leaves him with 32 years—that's 11,680 days.

One third of the remaining time he spends going from one place to another. That leaves only 21 years, which is 7,665 days to invest for eternity.

Believe it or not, the average, American male will spend nine years watching TV, movies, sporting events, playing video games, etc. That leaves 12 years or 4,380 days.

By age 36, only half this time remains, which is 6 years. You now have 2,190 days to invest your time wisely, and then, face the judgement bar of God to give an account for what you did with your life.

The most precious thing you have is not money—it's your eternal soul. You can always get more money; you cannot buy more time or, replay your life. Life is not a dress rehearsal. Hebrews 9:27 says,

> It is appointed unto a man once to die and then the judgment.

Eph. 5:15-17 says, "So be careful how you live. Don't live like fools, but like those who are wise. Make the most of every opportunity in these evil days."

How Much is Your Time Worth?

What is a year worth? Ask a graduate student who just failed a grade.

How much is a month worth? Ask a mother who has just given birth to a premature baby.

What is the value of a week? Ask the editor of a weekly newspaper.

What is the value of an hour? Ask young lovers waiting to meet.

What is the value of a minute? Ask someone who just missed a plane.

What is the value of a second? Ask someone who just missed what would have been a fatal accident.

What is the value of a millisecond? Ask someone who just won a silver medal at the Olympics!

Another reason people reject God is the fear of death. Most people don't want to think about death or sin or its consequences, so they live like they're never going to die. In 1 Cor. 15:55, the Bible says,

Death has no sting and the grave has no victory.

For the Christian, death isn't the end; it's the glorious beginning!

One of the distinguishing marks of a genuine work of God's Spirit in your life is simply this: sin will no longer be fun. You will want to obey the Lord because you love Him. Our obedience is not the obedience of a slave but of a loving child who has a perfect heavenly Father.

What Do I Do Now?

1. Pray. Talk to God as a child would speak to a loving father. This conversation is called prayer. There are many different kinds of prayer. In this case, it's a simple, child-like, personal, private conversation with God.

Talking to God is one of the most normal, natural, sane, rational, intelligent and wonderful things a human being can do. You don't even have to speak out loud. He knows your every thought. He wants to hear from and speak with you. One of the main ways God "speaks" is when we mediate on His Word. That is how He opens our understanding and imparts wisdom. To know the Word of God is to know the mind of God.

You can start by meditating on the principles found in this model prayer in Matthew 6:9-13,

> Our Father who art in heaven, holy be Thy name. Thy kingdom come, Thy will be done on earth as it is in heaven. Give us this day our daily bread. And forgive us our trespasses as we forgive those who have trespassed against us. And lead us not into temptation, but deliver us from evil. For Thine is the kingdom and the power and the glory forever. Amen.

Take time to think about the implications of each word and phrase in this prayer. It's practically inexhaustible. The very first word speaks to one of our greatest needs—the need to be free from selfishness. Meditating on God's Word is how spiritual truth is revealed to those who truly seek Him.

Contrary to popular opinion, as the first phrase in this prayer demonstrates, prayer is not primarily about getting God to give you what you want. It's more about you learning what God wants from you. He already knows what you need and want.

Spiritually speaking, there is a direct correlation between how much truth you possess and the degree of freedom you enjoy. In John 8:32 Jesus said,

> You shall know the truth and the truth shall make you free.

Look up Revelation 5:8 and think about what prayer means to God. Also see Psalm 22:3.

2. Read the Bible every day. Prayer is how you talk to God, and reading the Bible is one way God talks to you. The better you know the Word of God, the better you know the God of the Word. And, the better you know His Word, the easier it is to discern His will. This is how you grow in virtue and in knowledge about God, and, His kingdom principles for abundant life.

Get a Bible. Read the central verse (John 3:16), remember what it says, then go to the beginning, and start reading at Genesis 1:1. Keep reading every day until you complete it. Genesis is fascinating, and most of it is fairly easy to understand. As you read through, don't worry about the parts you may not understand at first. It's the parts you do understand that will challenge, encourage, and instruct you for successful living.

The more you study the Bible, the more you grow spiritually. The more you grow spiritually, the closer you get to God. Paradoxically, the closer you get to Him, the farther away you realize you are, and the closer you want to be. It's a glorious journey!

3. Make friends with other believers. The Bible calls this *fellowship*. Find a church that believes and teaches the Bible as the inerrant Word of God, and where the worship is inspiring. Then get involved!

Many churches have small groups that meet in homes during the week. This is almost always a great place to meet new friends and grow in your faith. Most of them are very nice people who are genuinely interested in helping you grow closer to God.

I cannot overemphasize the value of walking with like-minded people who will help you on your pilgrimage to spiritual growth and eternal life. Proverbs 13:20 says,

> Walk with wise men and you will become wise, but the companion of fools will be destroyed.

4. Learn how to share your faith. That is what this book is all about. Then, find people who are involved in front line ministry, and go with them—regularly. You'll never regret it throughout all eternity. Sharing God's plan of salvation with the lost and dying is the Great Commission to every Christian. Your marching orders are found in Matthew 28:19.

If you're worried about rejection, look up the following verses: 1 Peter 4:14, Luke 6:22-23, and Daniel 12:3. Leading someone to Christ is one of the most exciting things you could ever do!

Our website has helpful resources that will equip you to grow in your most holy faith. Go to: www.voice-wilderness.org.

Three Things We All Need

For man to be satisfied (free from insignificance), he needs three things: something to do, someone to love (and be loved by), and something to hope for.

All three of these life essentials are found in a personal love relationship with our great God and Savior, the Lord Jesus Christ.

I remember listening to a lecture by a Christian speaker on a college campus. After the message one student asked,

How do I know I exist?

To which the speaker replied,

Who should I say is asking?

Everyone laughed.

When you know who created you, you find the purpose for which you were designed. You are the crowning achievement of God's creation (He made you in His image and in His likeness).

As such, you are the supreme object of His love and affection, that is why Jesus died for you. It's not because you earned it; it's because He loves you. No matter what you have done, God is ready, willing, and able to forgive your sin on one condition—repentance. But you must do it while you still have breath. Time is running out!

Leaving A Legacy

When life is over and you are standing before the judgment bar of God, at that point many of the things that once seemed so important in this life will be loss. It will not matter where you were born, when you were born, who your parents were, your skin color, gender, or economic status. It's not what you bought, but what you built that will count. It's not how much you made, but how much you gave, not how much you learned but how much you taught. It's not competence but character that will count. It won't matter how many people you knew but how many people knew you because of your love for Christ. Every act of love, integrity, humility, compassion, courage, or sacrifice that enriched, empowered, or encouraged others to live for Christ, that is what will matter then—and for all eternity! [2]

Chicken Little Vs. Jesus Christ

Chicken Little was a little chicken who made the big time with a prophecy of doom and gloom. His mantra was straight and to the point,

The sky is falling, the sky is falling!

With the looming threat of nuclear Armageddon and World War III, terrorism, war in the Middle East, and the reality of corruption in government and business, the collapse of the US economy, earthquakes, famine, floods, fuel shortages, droughts, hurricanes, pandemics, emerging diseases, violence in the streets, immorality, organized crime, propaganda in the media, broken families, alcoholism, drug addiction, unemployment, apostasy in the church, Christianity becoming criminalized, and much, much more, I understand why "we the people" are very concerned about the future.

Humanly speaking, we have great reason to be troubled. But, spiritually speaking, we have even greater reason not to be.

Here are the words of the Master Himself from John 14: 1-3,

> Let not your heart be troubled; you believe in God, believe also in Me. In My Father's house are many mansions; if it were not so, I would have told you. I go to prepare a place for you. And if I go and prepare a place for you, I will come again and receive you to Myself; that where I am, there you may be also.

OUR BLESSED HOPE

And behold, I am coming quickly, and My reward is with Me, to give to every one according to his work. I am the Alpha and the Omega, the Beginning and the End, the First and the Last. Blessed are those who do His commandments that they may have the right to the tree of life, and may enter through the gates into the city.

—Jesus Christ from Revelation 22:12-14

Discussion Questions for Chapter One

1. You have only two choices: either _____ is eternal and uncreated, or _____ is eternal and uncreated. What terms correctly fill each blank?

2. Why must something be eternal?

3. What are the three main components of Einstein's Theory of Relativity, and how do they appear to fit Genesis 1:1?

4. Why is asking, "Where did God come from?" a nonsensical question?

5. What would be a better question to ask?

6. What most impresses you about the wonders of creation?

7. Read Psalm 19:1-3. What is God saying in these verses?

8. Read Romans 1:18-20. What does this passage mean, and what are its implications?

9. How might you reword Psalm 19:1-3 into a prayer of praise and thanksgiving to God?

10. What do you think God would have you do as a result of studying this chapter?

Discussion Questions for Chapter Two

1. Name three things that make the Bible unique.

2. Name three things that make Jesus unique.

3. How do we see the absolutes of evil, justice, forgiveness, truth, and love defined and reconciled on the cross of Christ?

4. How was love demonstrated on the cross? Can you think of any Scripture verses that speak to this?

5. Read John 4:24. What is meant by this verse?

6. Read the second part of John 16:2. How is this prophecy being fulfilled today?

7. What is so ironic about the Roman Empire falling and Christianity rising?

8. How is modern-day Israel a fulfillment of prophecy, and where do you see this in the Bible?

9. What do you think Jeremiah 31:35-36 means?

10. What are the implications of Bible prophecy being fulfilled? What should our response be?

Discussion Questions for Chapter Three

1. What evidence do we have that the Ten Commandments were written by God and not by man?

2. The Ten Commandments can be summed up and restated positively by two commands; what are they?

3. Look at Romans 13:8-10. What do the Ten Commandments have to do with love?

4. Read Romans 7:7. What role do the Ten Commandments play in showing us our need of salvation? Also see Galatians 3:24.

5. Look up Romans 2:15. What does this mean, and what is the implication for the whole world?

6. In Exodus 31, we are told that God etched the Ten Commandments in stone. What does "etched in stone" convey?

7. Look up Matthew 5:21 and 5:27. What do these commandments have in common, and what are we to learn from them (there is a hint in Romans 7:12-14)?

8. Look up Matthew 5:19. What does this mean?

9. Look up Matthew 19:16-21. What point is Jesus trying to make to the rich young ruler, and why does He omit the tenth commandment?

10. What do you think God would have you do as a result of the information in this lesson?

Discussion Questions for Chapter Four

1. What most impressed you about this lesson?

2. How does this lesson help you understand the Trinity?

3. In light of Exodus 3:14, what does John 6:24 mean and how might this relate to the Trinity?

4. Look up Mark 4:39, John 1:1-3; 1:14; 2:19-21; 8:58, 10:30; 14:9, 20:28, and Colossians 1:15-18. What are these verses saying? Now compare John 8:24 to Exodus 3:14. What do we learn?

5. What does it mean to "live in light of eternity"?

6. Read Matthew 5:13. How many effects of salt can you name, and how do they relate to what Jesus wants us to do?

7. Salt doesn't do anything until it does what? How is light different?

8. Look up Psalm 90:12. What does this mean?

9. Compare Exodus 4:11 to Luke 7:21. What is important, besides the fact that blind people gained sight?

10. Based on the first three chapters of this book, what are the three strongest arguments for faith in God?

Discussion Questions for Chapter Five

1. What is the difference between macroevolution and microevolution?

2. Has macroevolution ever been observed in a laboratory or anywhere else? If not, how does that affect the credibility of those who claim that evolution is a scientific fact?

3. What did Charles Darwin say concerning the fossil record and his theory? After 150 years of collecting fossils, what support does the record provide for his theory?

4. According to Romans 1:18-20, what do some people do with what they know in their hearts to be true? Why do they do it?

5. According Lee Strobel, what is one of the main reasons that cause people to deny the existence of God?

6. According to the well-known atheist Aldous Huxley, what is another reason people have for denying the existence of God?

7. Look up Psalm 14:1. What is the condition of this person's heart?

8. Look up Proverbs 18:2. Why might this be true of some people?

9. Why are some scientists afraid to admit publicly that they are creationists?

10. Why are some people afraid to openly love God? Check out Proverbs 29:25 for one possible answer. How do you think it makes God feel when His own people are ashamed of the Gospel? Now see Luke 9:26. What does Jesus mean there? Discuss the implications of Matthew 10: 28.

Discussion Questions for Chapter Six

1. What does God's most holy and proper name mean?

2. What impact should that have on us?

3. How do we know God is a Person rather than an obscure power or impersonal force?

4. Can a human being know God personally? Is it possible to cultivate a relationship with God?

5. Look up Romans 8:16. Has anyone in the group experienced this? If yes, please share it with the group.

6. Can people really know they are going to heaven, and how would they know? Look up Romans 8:16 and 1 John 5:13. What do these verses mean?

7. In the context of knowing God, what is the difference between intellectual assent and heart knowledge? How can you illustrate this difference?

8. Look up John 10:27-30. What principles are being taught?

9. What does God want you to do in light of everything we have covered in these lessons?

10. Reword that answer into a prayer.

Suggested Reading

1. *I Don't Have Enough Faith To Be An Atheist*
   —Norman Geisler

2. *Jesus Christ The Master Evangelist—How to Present the Gospel the Way Jesus Did*
   —Philip DelRe

3. *The Power of God From Sinai to the Cross*—Audio CD
   —Philip DelRe

4. *Hell's Best Kept Secret*
   —Ray Comfort

5. *Evidence That Demands a Verdict*
   —Josh McDowell

6. *The Fear of Man Vs. The Fear of God*
   —Philip DelRe

7. *One Heartbeat Away*
   —Mark Cahill

8. *The Evidence Bible*
   —Ray Comfort

Suggested Websites

1. www.voice-wilderness.org

2. www.answersingenesis.org

3. www.roncarlson.com

4. www.livingwaters.com

5. www.gal416.org

Voice in the Wilderness Ministries has other helpful resources available on our website. Be sure to visit us at *www.voice-wilderness.org.*

This book is available in bulk. We also have a Gospel tract that is a miniature of this book entitled *God's Three Witnesses.* You can download a free copy on our website.

Dr. David Larsen is Professor Emeritus of Preaching at Trinity Evangelical Divinity School in Deerfield, Illinois. He said ours is the finest Gospel tract he has seen.

Phil speaks at pastors' conferences, men's retreats, youth rallies, schools, churches, and prisons across the country and around the world.

If you would like to book Phil for a speaking engagement, call: 815-547-0765.

End Notes

Chapter Two: The Word of God, Living and Written

1. Quoted in Josh McDowell, *Evidence that Demands a Verdict* (San Bernardino, CA: Here's Life Publishers, Inc., 1972), pp.191-192.

Chapter Five: Evolution Is Not Science, It's Monkey Mythology

1. Darwin: *Origin of the Species*. P.143.

2. Ibid., 144.

3. Ibid., 149.

4. Ibid., 230.

5. Ibid., 342.

6. Randall Niles, *"Problems with the Fossil Record,"* All About the Journey *www.all-aboutthejourney.org/problems-with-the-fossil-record.html.*

7. Lawrence O. Richards, *It Couldn't Just Happen* (Thomas Nelson, Inc., 1989), pp.139-140.

8. Aldous Huxley, *Ends and Means*, 1937.

9. Lee Strobel; Radio Interview on Moody Radio.

10. G.K. Chesterton, *The Quotable Chesterton*.

Chapter Six: Who is God?

1. Photo of Cordillera del Paine, a mountain in Chile, is courtesy of the PBH Network.

2. Adapted from the DVD on the Gerson Therapy for cancer.